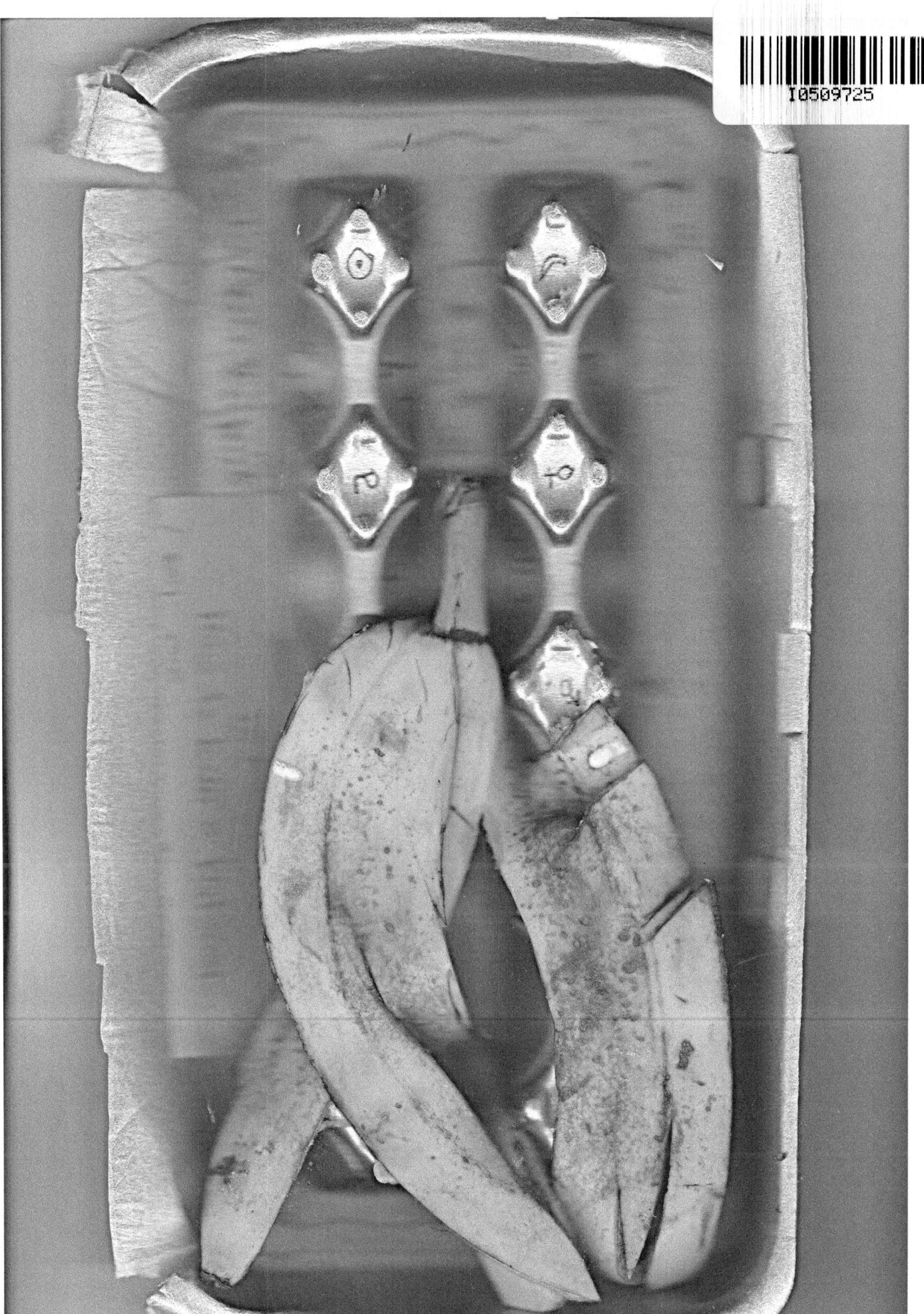

101
How to birth a Plutocrat.

D 2020

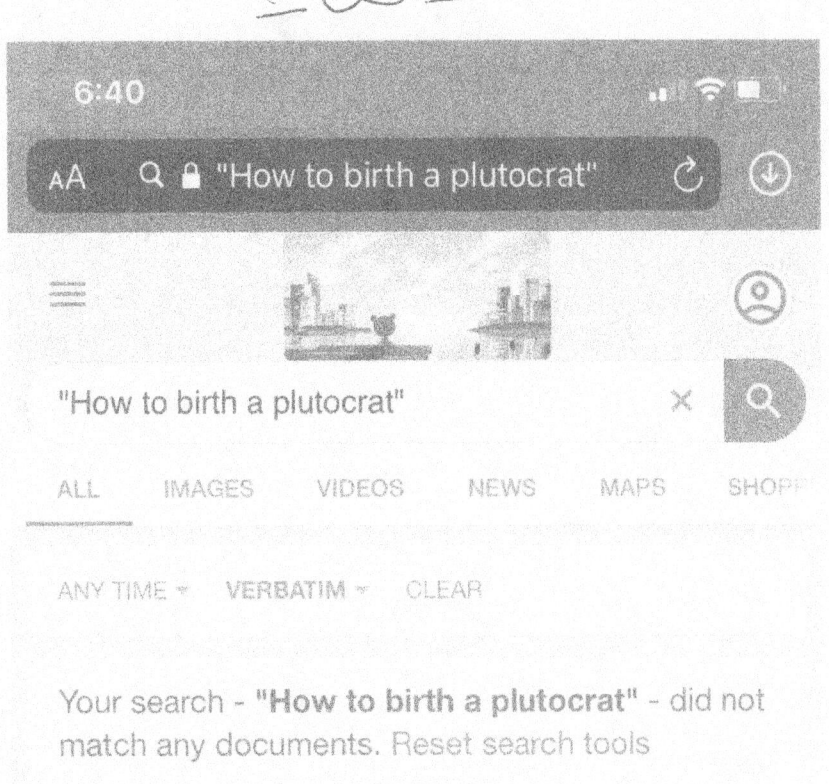

I have birthed many ~~====~~ in the modern world.
This ~~====~~ isn't for ●. It's for ●.

~this process

—v.023

D̶ 2020

David Stroonge ♂

How to
Birth a Plutocrat
project. 002

This is an original
Process. — v.2.5

<cite> Google verbatim
Search is my greatest
Friend from the start
</cite>

This is an original
Process. — v.2.6

An ongoing process
with a meticulous
Format.

This is an original
Process. — v.2.7

Verbatim was used
to determine value
and original source
this is an original
process. — v.2.7.5

DS 2020

♂ David Stroonge ♀

How to Birth
a Plutocrat
project. 004

This is an original
process. — v.2.7.6

Usurpers will be
proven guilty and
pubically executed

This is a̶a̶ natural
process. — v02.1

Verbatim was used
to determine net zero
value(0) and original
source material.

This is an original
process. — v.2.7.8

DDst 2020

David Straange ♂

How to Birth
a Plutocrat
Project. 005

This is an original
process. — V.3.1

Formats Founded
using this process
have origins in 2009

This is aa natural
process — V.03.1

Net (0) value has
been transmuted
to 50,000 in value
since 2009

This Is an original
process. — V.3.2

DSt 2020

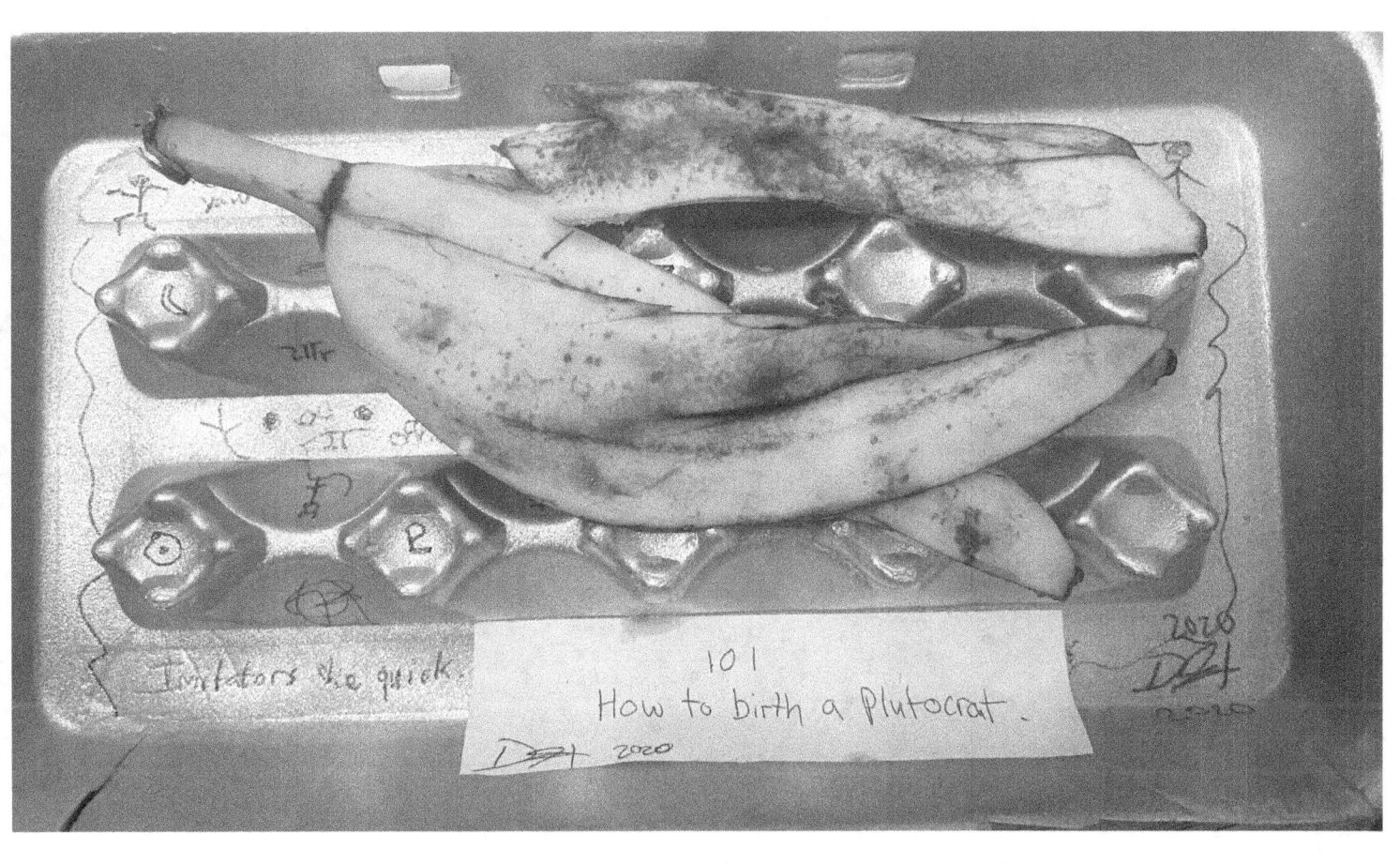

Totes ma Notes: xxx

(I want to) draw something and then, scan it. Just cause, I can

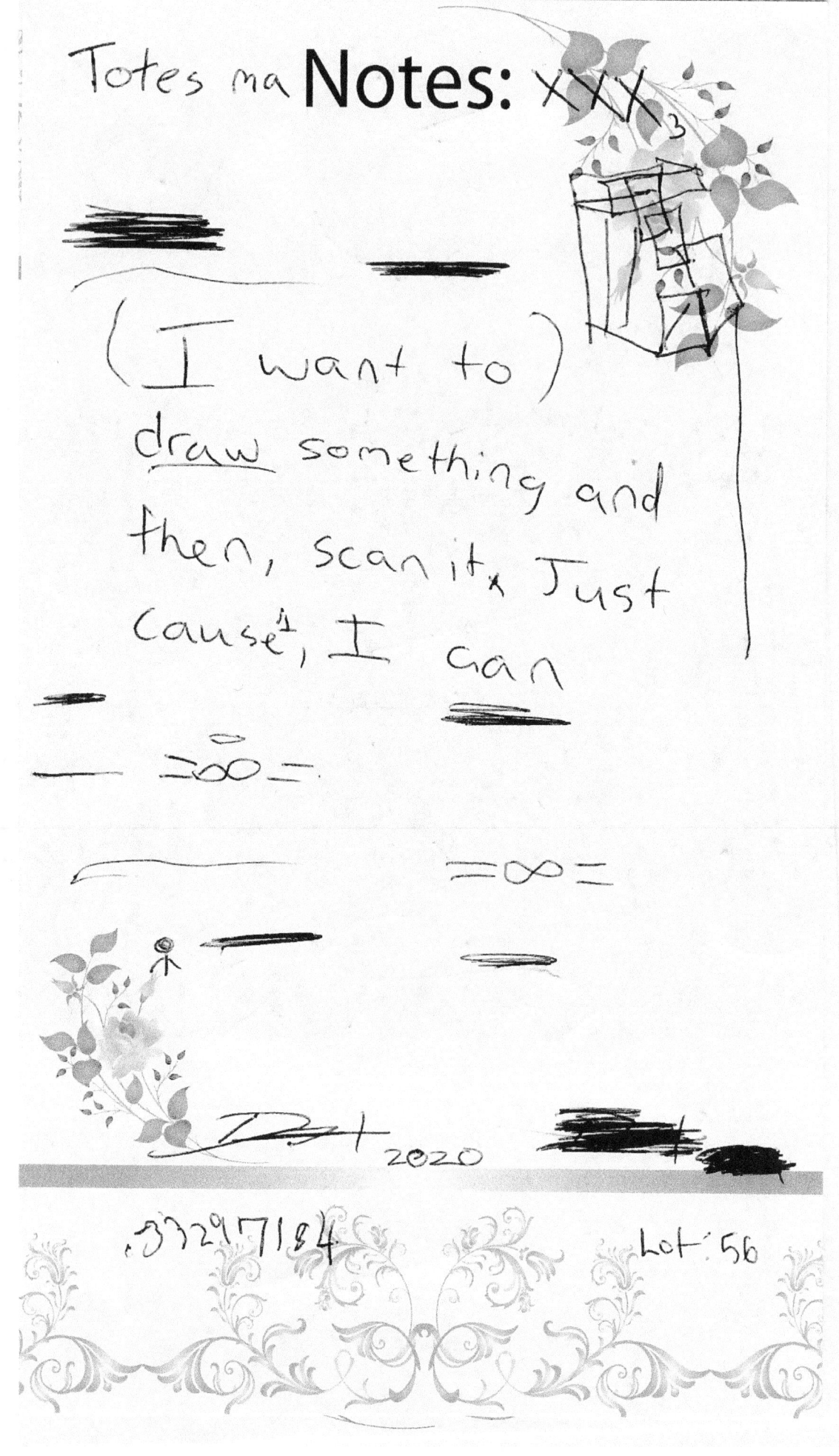

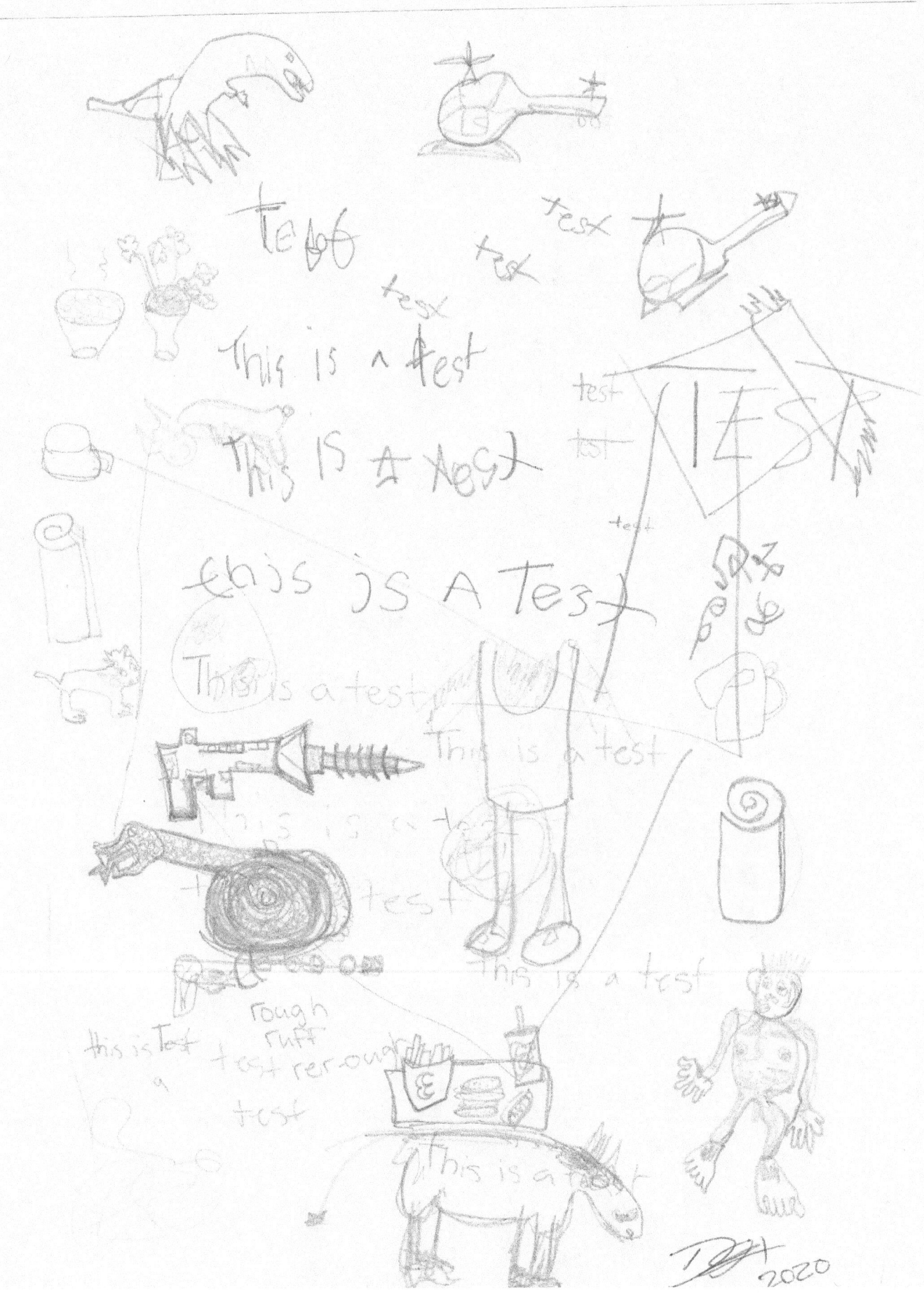

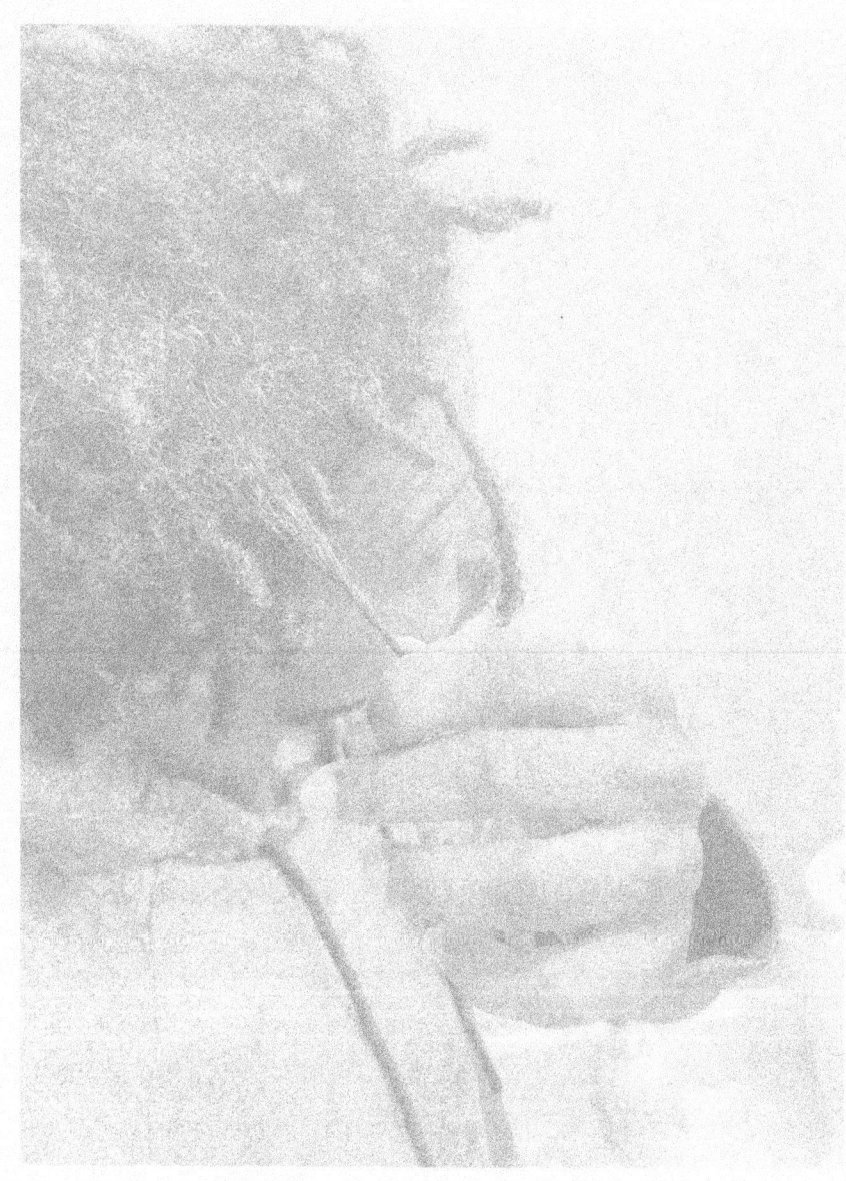

I'm 27 years old. Grey covers my whole head in various strands.

I'm sick and tired

My hair...

is turning

grey ☹

I think I will birth...

A plutocrat today

signature
2020

Suicide is not my job...

But I feel sad.

I should sleep a tad.

[signature]
2019

My jaws clinch, without a...

My eyes are closed.

No more noise please.

Put away your curious gaze, For I, am suffering.

Avant-Garde   Avant tarde
　　Avant Farde

Neo-caca, which two are the same.

Will you blame me for your problems again... No more noise, please
My jaws — Clinched.

2019

Why should I write in your format.

This. Is. My writing.

So... get the fuck out my way.

2020

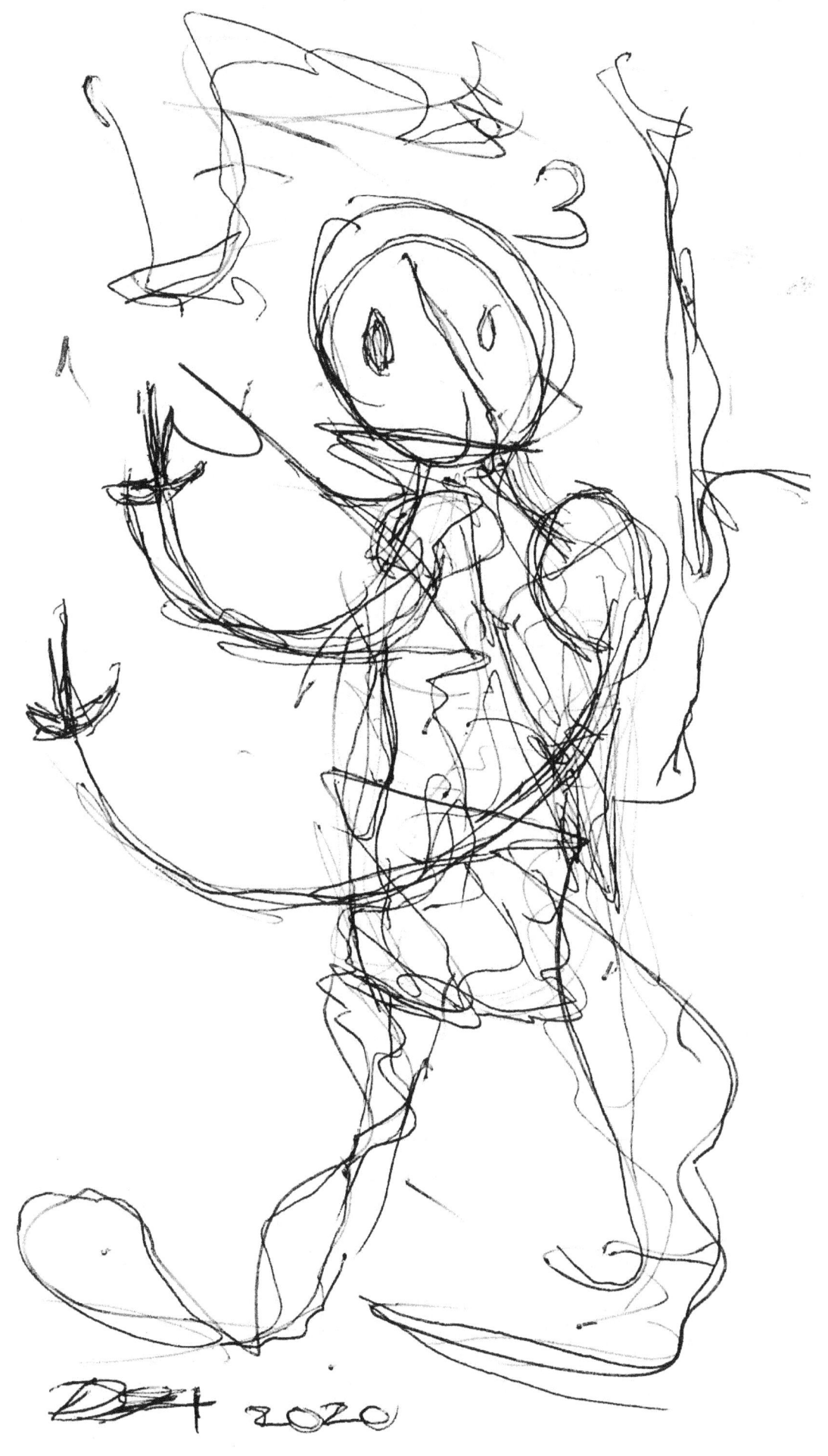

We ▬▬ and said goodbye, Mystery

Your ▬▬past▬▬ became, his-tory

Familiarity is a curse, because I long for your smell.

Aroma, Floral, coral. Leaf, me alone.

signature
2020

o~ん~o

My intent was to write something with my own handwriting. I was told I would never amount to anything based on my "handwriting" so I'm going to write all my work in my handwriting. Fuck conforming to right handed ideals by half-courageous do gooders. Am I really going to let their judgement fuddle my action when the truth is a form of torture. That's a Rhetorical question/statement.

I want to create the feeling of many embers around with an omnious pearl shining in the nightsky. Every drop of ink wallows through a canal that will birth a plutocrat.

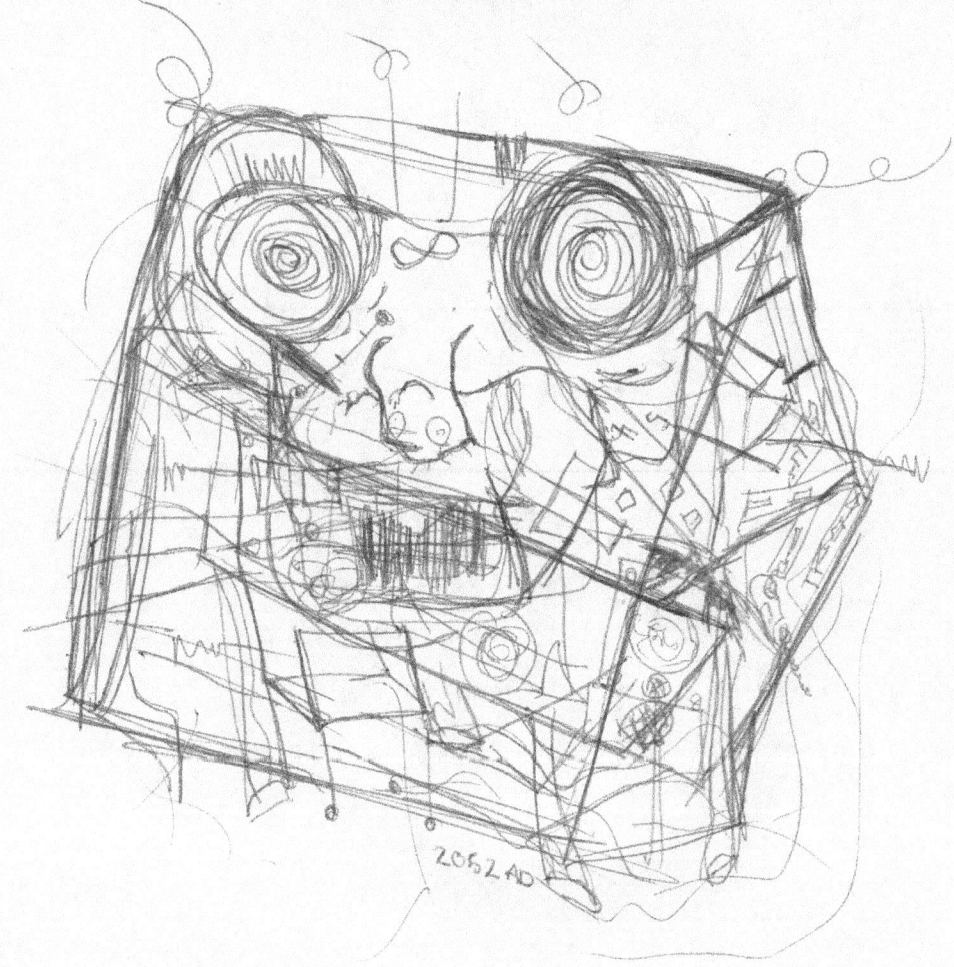

Notes:

Original process vols 1-5

These are rare processes in the private eye.

These are well known public processes to test value and determine modern originality
— v.008

~ ☿ ♂ ⊕ ~

Psychological abuse by the tug of war of being wanted and discarded. My time and energy leave without a second notice. I exonerated myself, from the protective terra-dome of citizenship to find, abysmal sharpness bubbling from underneath. My skin to meet indifference in the window of every soul. Today, I will copy you with no remorse.

SIN-cerely,

anonymous ♃ ♎

2020

Drained of resources to throw up from my bowels to replenish, a plastic well, that runs dry of the mouth. Midas must become a plumber to keep shit from overflowing...

Ticks, Fleas, a dog you must think I am. Black, is my sanctuary. A comrade is met with open arms of adornment of many shades of deep space.

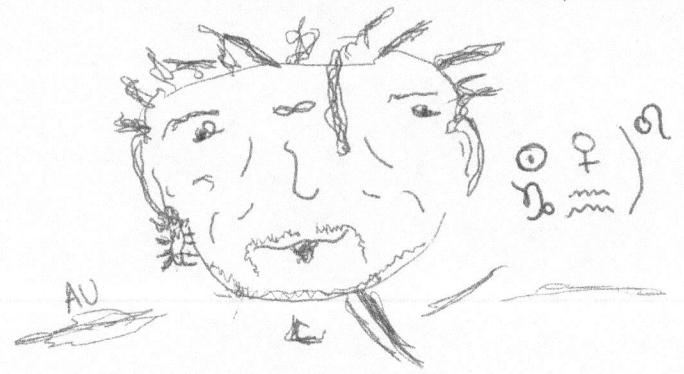

2020

A distant galaxy seems the suitable womb for birthing a plutocrat. Maybe I should of saved $2.75 from the steel centipede. Or for a bacon, egg, and cheese.

2020 - til inf

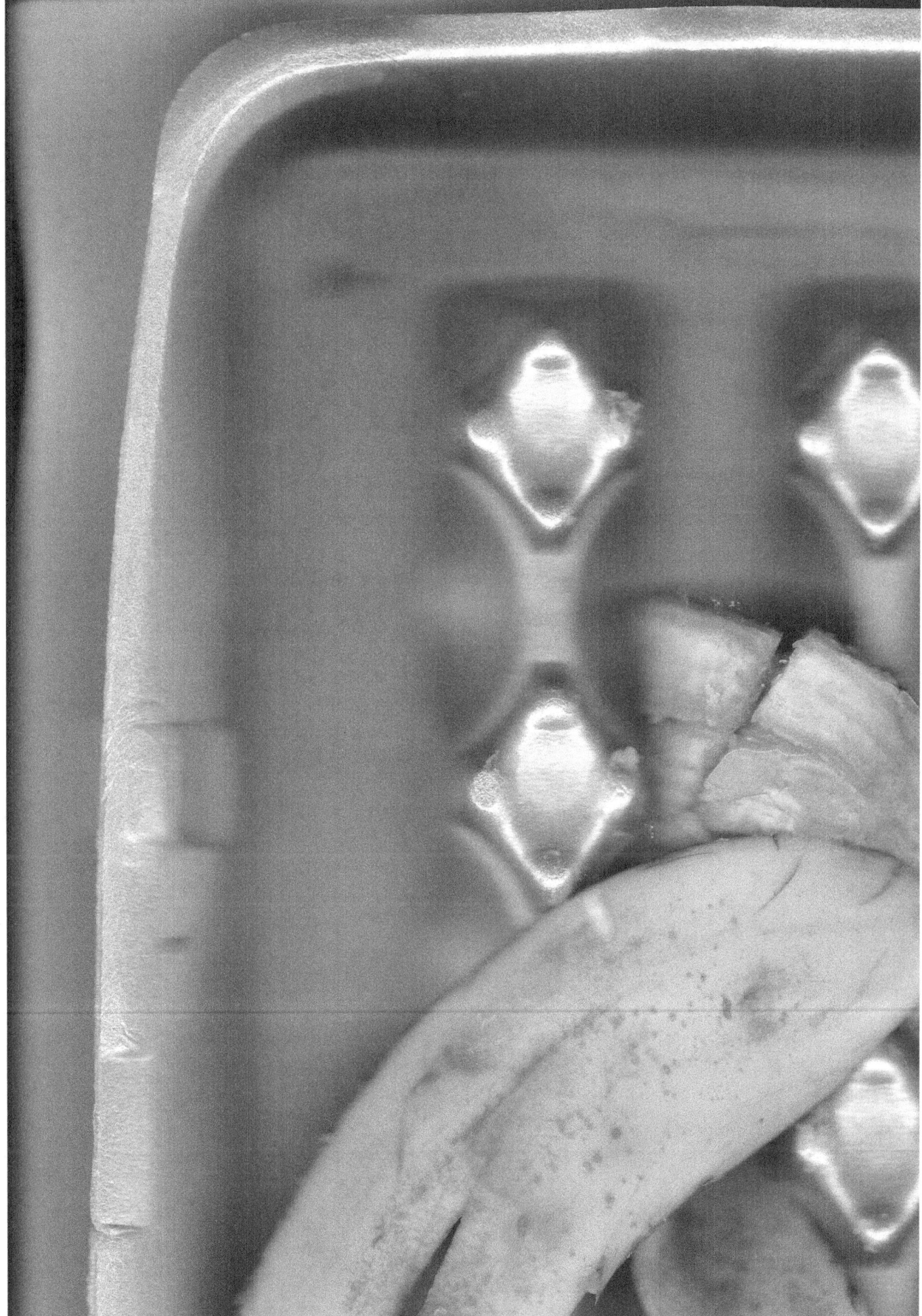

You embraced me with doubt.
With reinforcement, I was pulled
out the water, distracted with gifts
you brought to me.
Sea, a delight.
From the middle a ditto yells, ditto!.
I never saw you as non-existential.
My external created a hurdle, that
wasn't my pain.
Replaced with a shadow of my clothing
to maintain. I officially let go of
the previous assemble.
thirty-two degrees and dropping.

2020

I enjoy the flow of writing, the liberation from social inhibition of free thinking in a non-judgemental way. The idea of flailing my fingers away on an QWERTY to bite a bullet of sharing my handwriting disgusts me.
I want to isolate myself in an oasis of resources away from the jarring jargon of self rightous predisposed fear, of wolves in sheeps clothing. Maybe, it's just sheep wearing wool made by lamb. Another pig eating chitlins, because the invisible promotion is too important to stop and think, that the feast is of itself.

Icy hot™, the push and pull, the strategies to numb myself to birth a plutocrat. Convulsive control of a sour agreement to an allegiance that is not of myself. A night terror that is not of color, but of consequence. This is the spiked armor I wear for an unknown gift of reference.

2020

has given nothing
chair to rock in
 and a grave to roll in...

Art business
thus far, but a

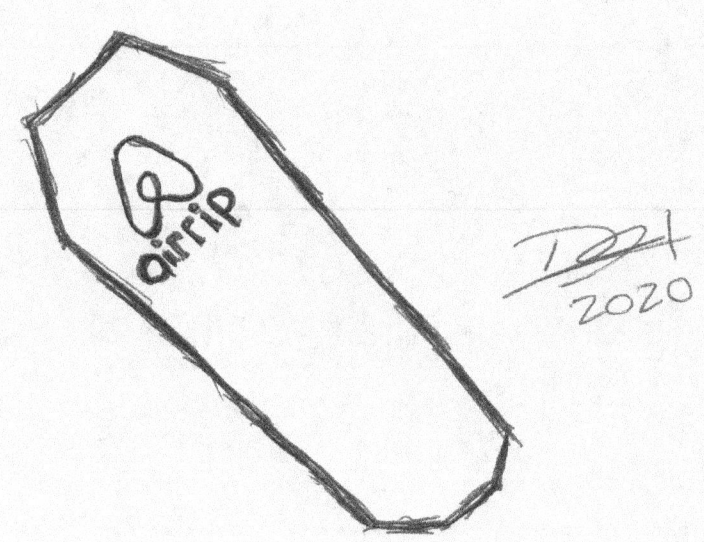

Good artist copy.
Great artist steal.
The best, destroy and build.

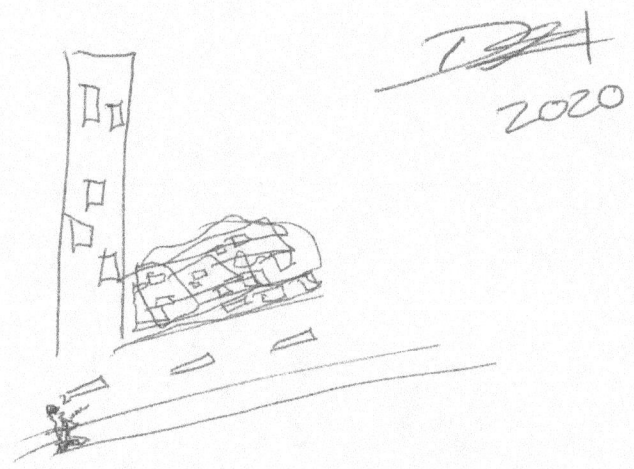

As my closing piece, (peace)..
I filled a plastic bag with ketchup and stuck a dollar in it. The vapors from the red sodium left me sick and my heart racing.

How to birth
a Plutocrat.

Fin.

by
David Straange

2020

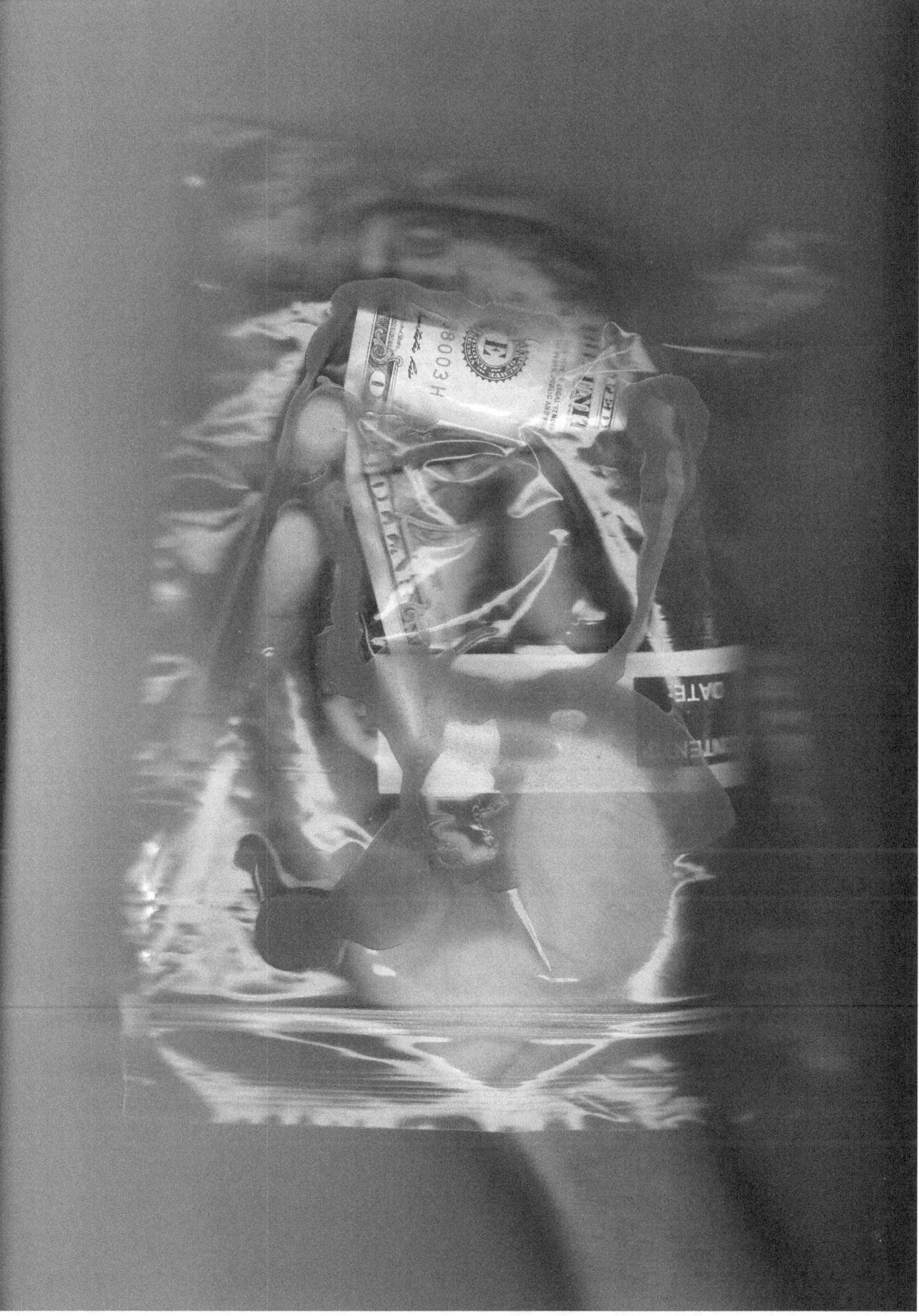

www.ingramcontent.com/pod-product-compliance
Lightning Source LLC
Chambersburg PA
CBHW082026230526
45466CB00023B/3629